# 50 NIFTY TRAVEL GAMES

## Written by Kevin Taylor and Joan C. Taylor
## Illustrated by Neal Yamamoto

Lowell House
Juvenile
Los Angeles

**Contemporary Books**
Chicago

NOTE: The numbered suitcases in the upper right-hand corner of each project indicates the level of difficulty; 1 being the easiest and 3 the hardest.

PLAYER NOTE: If a game needs a certain number of players to work, it is stated under "What You'll Need." If the number of players is not mentioned, it means the game or activity can be played alone or with any number of people.

Project Editor: Amy Downing
Design: Dalton Design


Library of Congress Catalog Card Number: 94-2251

ISBN: 1-56565-108-1

10 9 8 7 6 5 4 3

# GET READY FOR YOUR ADVENTURE!

In this book you'll find all sorts of great activities to enjoy in a car, in a plane, on a train, on a boat, or however you're traveling! But before you leave, here are a few things you'll need to do to prepare for your trip.

## WHAT YOU'LL NEED

- shoe box
- foil or wrapping paper
- scissors
- sheet of plain paper
- tape
- markers
- glue
- game supplies for trip
- flat board or lap desk (optional)

## BEFORE YOU LEAVE

**1** Flip through the pages of this book. Some of the activities you'll find are things you can do without needing any supplies—word games, sing-alongs, and many more. Others require a few simple supplies, such as pencils, pens, rulers, crayons, scissors, glue, and tape. Collect some of the items for these games and activities *right now!*

**2** Grab your shoe box. Cover the box with foil or wrapping paper by taping it to the box. Do the same with the lid. On a separate piece of paper, write with a marker, "TRAVEL SUPPLIES: PROPERTY OF (your name). DO NOT DISTURB!!" Then, glue this to the side of your travel box. When the box is dry, put all the supplies that you've collected inside.

**3** If you're traveling by car, you may want to bring along a lap desk or a flat board made of wood for a work space. This will make the crafts easier to make and the games easier to play. But remember, with or without a lap desk, never use scissors or other sharp objects when you're zipping along in a moving vehicle. It could be dangerous. So, whenever you see the box below, it means to do your cutting *before* you leave on your trip!

> **Never use scissors in a moving vehicle, especially a car, bus, or train. Cut out what you need before you leave.**

## BON VOYAGE!

# LIVE! FROM THE ROAD

**PARENTAL SUPERVISION REQUIRED**

Ever wanted to be a reporter and interview all sorts of people? Or do your own weather report or travelogue? Here's your chance to do it all!

## WHAT YOU'LL NEED

• portable tape recorder with batteries    • pencil or pen    • notepad
• small microphone (optional)    • blank cassette tape

## HOW TO PLAY

**1**   Grab the tape recorder and put in a blank tape. Most tape recorders have built-in microphones, but you may want to use a small microphone for a clearer sound.

**2**   Decide exactly what you want to record. Do you want to hold an interview or give a straight newscast? Here are a few ideas:

• Interview your family and friends about the trip.
• Interview people you meet along the way about their trips or home towns.
• Do a newscast from the car, plane, ship, or hotel, reporting on all the most recent happenings on board or in the area.
• Start a diary with dates, times, weather reports, and your observations about the trip.

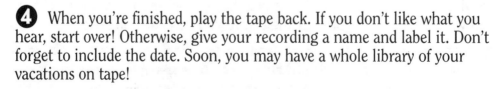

**3**   Before you start interviewing anyone, write down a few questions so you'll be prepared. If you are interviewing someone you don't know, stay with a parent at all times. *Never go anywhere alone with a stranger.*

**4**   When you're finished, play the tape back. If you don't like what you hear, start over! Otherwise, give your recording a name and label it. Don't forget to include the date. Soon, you may have a whole library of your vacations on tape!

## ONE STEP FURTHER

Incorporate silly commercials in-between your interviews—be creative!

# TRUNKS, EARS, AND TAILS

Can't decide who gets the front seat? The window seat? The last soda? Here's a surefire and fun way to settle all your traveling disputes. It makes a good game, too.

## WHAT YOU'LL NEED

• two or more players

## HOW TO PLAY

**1** The next time you and your brother or sister can't stop bickering, look at each other, shake hands, and say, "Trunks, Ears, and Tails."

**2** Then both of you make a fist, pound it into your other hand once as you both say "Trunks." Pound your fists again and say "Ears," and pound your fists a third time as you both say "Tails."

**3** On the third pound (the "Tails" pound), each of you does one of three things:

• Put out your index finger, meaning "Trunk," (which stands for the trunk on an elephant).
• Put out your index finger and your middle finger, meaning "Ears," (which stands for a cat's ears).
• Put out your pinky finger, meaning "Tail," (which stands for a mouse's tail).

**4** How do you decide the winner? Easy! The elephant can step on the cat, so the elephant wins out over the cat. The cat can catch the mouse, so the cat wins out over the mouse. And since mice can spook elephants, the mouse wins out over the elephant!

# ROCKY MOUNTAIN TREASURE TUMBLE

Make it down the mountain with your hidden treasure—but don't fall off the edge, or you'll lose both your riches and the game!

## WHAT YOU'LL NEED

- cardboard
- ruler
- scissors
- pens, pencils, markers, or crayons
- seven bobby pins
- tape
- penny

> **Never use scissors in a moving vehicle, especially a car, bus, or train. Cut out what you need before you leave.**

## BEFORE YOU LEAVE

Use a ruler to cut the cardboard to playing size, which is 6 by 11 inches. Now you're ready to prepare the game board, which can be done before you leave or while traveling.

## PREPARING YOUR GAME BOARD

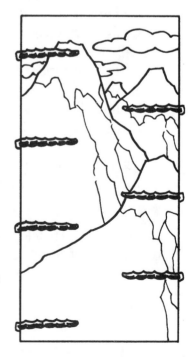

**1** Make sure your cardboard is in a vertical position. Then draw a huge mountain on the cardboard piece using pens, pencils, markers, or crayons.

**2** Now clip your bobby pins onto the cardboard in the positions shown. The ridged side of the bobby pins should be on the front of the game board. With tape, secure the bobby pins to the back of the cardboard. These will be your "footholds" for your challenging mountain descent.

**3** Draw a flag and write "Start" above the top left bobby pin. Then draw a small house with the word "Home" above the bottom left bobby pin. Finally, draw a treasure chest above each of the rest of the bobby pins, close to the edge of the cardboard. Write the number 10 inside each treasure chest and inside the house.

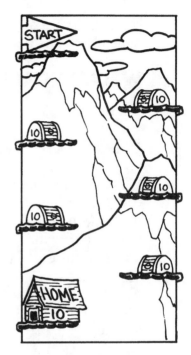

## HOW TO PLAY

**1** Now that your game board is complete, place a penny at "Start" and turn on your imagination. That penny is you, and your goal is to reach "Home" and pick up as many treasure points as you can along the way.

**2** Pick your way down the treacherous path by gently tilting the board from side to side. You will drop to the next foothold. There you will discover a hidden treasure. Each time you safely make it (by covering each treasure with your penny), you receive 10 points.

**3** If you fall off the mountain (the game board), you must start back up at the top. You lose all the treasure points you've earned, along with an additional minus 10 points. The player with the most treasure points at the end of three turns wins.

## ONE STEP FURTHER

Add a monster to the game! Draw Bigfoot—the horrible, hairy monster of the Rockies—on your game board, and if your penny touches him, you automatically lose!

**5**

# 7-11 ZIP! ZAP!

Here's a game that will challenge your mind and twist your tongue. And remember—don't zip when you should zap!

## WHAT YOU'LL NEED

• two or more players

## HOW TO PLAY

**1** Get ready for fast action! To begin playing, every player takes a turn counting, beginning with the number 1 ("1-2-3" etc.). Easy, right? Here's the tricky part: When the count reaches 7, a multiple of 7 (like 14 or 28), or a number with 7 in it (like 17 or 27), the person whose turn it is has to say "zip!" instead of the number.

**2** To make things even more challenging, when the count reaches 11 or a multiple of 11 (like 22 or 33), the person whose turn it is says "zap!" instead.

**3** Ready for a practice? "1-2-3-4-5-6-zip!-8-9-10-zap!-12-13-zip!-15-16-zip!-18-19-20-zip!-zap!" And so on. Make sure everybody gets his or her turn—no skipping. Got it? Good!

**4** If you make a mistake on the number or on a "zip!" or a "zap!," you're out. The last one in wins. Now see how fast and how high you can count!

# VACATION CONCENTRATION

Are you "game" for a competition that will test your memory and concentration skills? Then get playing!

## WHAT YOU'LL NEED

- two or more players
- two shoe box tops
- ruler
- pen or pencil
- scissors

**Never use scissors in a moving vehicle, especially a car, bus, or train. Cut out what you need before you leave.**

## BEFORE YOU LEAVE

**1** With a ruler, divide each shoe box top equally into 20 squares (three lines long ways, four lines across).

**2** Trim off the edges of one shoe box top, then cut along the lines to create 20 game pieces. The second shoe box top is your game board.

**3** Write an "A" on two pieces, a "B" on two pieces, a "C" on two pieces, and so on down to "J." (You can write the letters while you're traveling if you want to.)

## HOW TO PLAY

**1** Turn the pieces facedown and mix them up. Place each piece facedown on the game board.

**2** Taking turns, flip over two pieces and look for a match. Keep the ones you match.

**3** The player with the most pairs at the end wins! A tie? Play again!

# "AND WHATCHA GONNA BRING?"

This alphabet game is especially fun with a large group. Once you get the hang of it, it's as easy as A-B-C!

## WHAT YOU'LL NEED

• two or more players

## HOW TO PLAY

**1** To begin, the first player says, "I'm going on down to the park." The other players respond, "And whatcha gonna bring?" The first player answers back, "I'm going on down to the park and I'm bringing an alligator" (or anything else that begins with the letter "A").

**2** Then the second player says, "I'm going on down to the park." The others ask, "And whatcha gonna bring?" The second player must repeat the "A" word, and then think of a "B" word. For example, the player might say: "I'm going on down to the park and I'm bringing an alligator and a baby" (or a baseball, bear, or banana).

**3** Then the next player takes his or her turn, repeating all the things that have gone before and naming something that begins with "C." Continue taking turns coming up with a word that begins with the next letter in the alphabet. If you can't remember all the things that went before, get them out of order, or can't think of a word that begins with the correct letter, then—you guessed it—you're out! And no fair writing the words down. This is a test of your memory! The last person in is the winner.

# 8 T-SHIRT TRAVELOGUE

## PARENTAL SUPERVISION REQUIRED

Have you ever wished you could break your leg just so you could get all your friends to sign your cast? Instead, have everyone you meet on your trip sign your shirt. You'll meet lots of new friends, and what's more, there's no pain involved!

## WHAT YOU'LL NEED

• old white T-shirt    • permanent pens or markers, various colors

## HOW TO PLAY

**1** First of all, choose a large T-shirt that your parents won't mind you marking up.

**2** Then, wherever you go on your trip, get everyone you meet to sign your shirt with his or her name and a message, using the permanent pen or marker. Ask food servers, hotel managers, tour guides, gas station attendants—anyone! When asking people to sign your shirt, stay with a parent at all times. *Never go anywhere alone with a stranger.*

**3** Give each person a different color marker to make your shirt as colorful as possible.

## ONE STEP FURTHER

For an extra twist and even nuttier memories, find only people whose names start with the same letter as the place you're visiting, such as "Andy from Anchorage" or "Beth from Berthoud."

# BLINDFOLDED DRAWING

Here's your chance to see what kind of silly pictures you can make in this hilarious game where your ears and your hand are the only "eyes" you have!

## WHAT YOU'LL NEED

- two or more players
- paper
- pen or pencil
- hard surface (optional)
- scarf, bandanna, or sock

## HOW TO PLAY

**1** Each player needs a piece of paper and a pen or pencil. If possible, put the paper on a hard surface.

**2** All players except for one should tie a blindfold (the scarf, bandanna, or sock) around their heads so they can't see anything. Now the one unblindfolded player should describe the passing scenery as accurately as possible. The "blind" players need to listen carefully and draw what is being described. No fair peeking!

**3** Compare drawings. Whose picture looks the most like the scenery you've passed? Whose looks most like a bunch of shapeless blobs? Let Mom or Dad be the judge!

**4** Play until every player has had a chance to describe the scenery.

# 10 VACATION AVIATION

Create super paper jets that you design and build while you're traveling, then test them at different stops along the way. See who builds the plane that flies the farthest, straightest, longest—and has the fewest collisions!

## WHAT YOU'LL NEED

- paper
- pen or pencil
- colored markers (optional)
- ruler
- watch with a second hand

## HOW TO PLAY

**1** First, create and build your very own paper airplane—make it as simple or as fancy as you want! With colored markers, draw designs such as flames or shooting stars on the sides and nose. Don't forget to give each plane a name.

**2** Make up a chart like the one pictured here. Remember to include statistics such as the flight number, plane name, date and time, weather conditions, flight distance, flight time (use a watch with a second hand), and any other important information.

**3** Now you're all set for the great plane race! Once your mom or dad stops the car (don't throw the planes in the car—they may never fly again if your parents get a hold of them!), everyone flies his or her plane and records the statistics on the chart. The plane that flies the furthest and for the longest amount of time wins! Don't just stop with one flight. Fly the planes several times to see which plane is the day's top flyer.

| FLIGHT NUMBER | PLANE NAME | DATE/TIME | WEATHER CONDITIONS | FLIGHT DISTANCE | FLIGHT TIME |
|---|---|---|---|---|---|
| 1 | SPARK PLUG | JUNE 2 9:20 AM | COLD, WINDY | 20 FEET | 17 SECONDS |
| 2 | SPARK PLUG | JUNE 2 9:22 AM | COLD, WINDY | 19 FEET | 15 SECONDS |
| 1 | SOPWITH CAMEL | JUNE 2 9:25 AM | COLD, WINDY | 14 FEET | 10 SECONDS |
| 2 | SOPWITH CAMEL | JUNE 2 9:28 AM | COLD, WINDY | 17 FEET | 13 SECONDS |
| 1 | RED BARON | JUNE 2 12 NOON | WARM, LIGHT BREEZE | 20 FEET | 16 SECONDS |
| 3 | SPARK PLUG | JUNE 2 12:02 PM | WARM, LIGHT BREEZE | 18 FEET | 14 SECON |
| 1 | PAPPY BOYNTON | JUNE 2 12:05 PM | WARM, LIGHT BREEZE | 17 FEET | |

# BIG ADVENTURE MINI-BOOK

This is a perfect way to record your trip! Create your own travel journal using paper, string, and your imagination.

## WHAT YOU'LL NEED

- 10 to 20 sheets of 8½-by-11-inch paper
- hole puncher
- string, three pieces about 6 inches long

- scissors
- pens or pencils
- glue
- tape

- postcards, leaves, napkins, and anything you find on your trip that you want to include

> **Never use scissors in a moving vehicle, especially a car, bus, or train. Cut out what you need before you leave.**

## BEFORE YOU LEAVE

**1** You'll want to get your book put together before you leave in case something interesting happens the moment your trip begins! To start, fold each sheet of paper in half, horizontally.

**2** Lay the open sheets on top of each other, then fold them all together so that the folds are on the left side. When you've got the sheets lined up, punch three holes along the left side, about ½ inch from the folded edge. You've got the beginnings of your travel book!

LAY SHEETS ON TOP OF EACH OTHER; FOLDS SHOULD BE ON LEFT SIDE.

**3** Now thread a piece of string through each of the holes and tie it carefully. Be gentle—make sure the paper doesn't get wrinkled or torn.

## HOW TO PLAY

Now you're ready to fill the book with travel mementos—anything you want to remember! Collect autographs, draw pictures of the places you visit, and write about funny things that happen on the trip. Also, tape or glue souvenirs in your book, such as napkins from restaurants, postcards, or unusual leaves from your favorite campgrounds or parks. Don't forget to label each page with the date and location. When you get home, you'll have a book full of memories—a terrific tale of your Big Adventure Vacation!

# MAGICAL MYSTERY PICTURES

Make your own magnificent work of art! How about a purple sun or orange grass? Even a neon green castle! You'll be amazed at your own creations!

## WHAT YOU'LL NEED

- paper
- pen or pencil
- crayons
- hard surface
- paper clip or coin

## HOW TO PLAY

**1** Draw an abstract design on a piece of paper.

**2** Color in all the parts of your design, using as many color crayons as you can. It is important to press down hard with your crayons, so find a sturdy surface to work on.

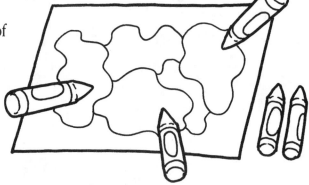

**3** Now completely cover the colorful design with black crayon. Rub really hard so you can't see *any* other color peeking through!

**4** Using an unfolded paper clip or the side of a coin, scratch out the picture of your choice by scraping off the black crayon. You can draw a picture of your pet or your family, or you may want to write your name in big block letters. Because you don't know the colors underneath the black crayon, you will be surprised by what appears. One note of caution: This game may result in black crayon smudges on the sides of your hands. Don't smear them on your face!

# LICENSE TO SPELL

This spelling game based on the license plates of passing cars definitely "spells" hours of fun for you and your traveling buddies.

## WHAT YOU'LL NEED

- three or more players
- paper
- pens or pencils
- passing cars

## HOW TO PLAY

**1** All the players decide on a subject, such as "Movies." Other category ideas include science fiction books, sports stars, cars, monsters, cartoon characters, dinosaurs, superheroes, and wild animals.

**2** Choose one player to be the "caller." You can rotate who the caller is every round or change callers every game.

**3** Ask the caller to call out all the letters from the license plate numbers of passing cars. Everybody else writes them down.

**4** The first player to spell the name of a title or object within the subject, using only the letters called out from the licence plates, wins the round. The winner gets a point for each letter used. You can use each letter only once. If two people come up with a word at the same time, whoever has the longest word (has used the most letters) wins that round. A game can be made up of anywhere from five to ten rounds or more!

17

# A-MAZE-ING PORTABLE PINBALL

**14**

You'll find out who has got the quickest reflexes and sharpest eye with this great travel maze game that you design, build, and play yourself!

## WHAT YOU'LL NEED

- shoe box top (use the one from your supply box)
- heavy cardboard (like the flaps from a packing box)
- 8½-by-11-inch construction paper
- scissors
- cotton balls
- glue
- pen or pencil
- paper clips
- marbles

> **Never use scissors in a moving vehicle, especially a car, bus, or train. Cut out what you need before you leave.**

## BEFORE YOU LEAVE

**1** Cut the piece of cardboard to fit snugly inside the shoe box top. This will be your game board. When you're ready to play the game, slip this piece of cardboard into your supply box lid.

**2** Cut the paper into four or five different sizes of rectangles, no bigger than 8 inches long.

## PREPARING YOUR GAME BOARD

**1** The object of this game is to get your marble through the maze game board that you create yourself. In your maze, you will create tunnels and arches that you must successfully go through, as well as bottomless holes and sandpits that you must avoid. Begin with your "Start" and "Finish." To make the "Start," roll a cut-out rectangle into a cylinder tunnel (it must be wide enough for your marble to fit through), glue the edges together, then glue it into the bottom right-hand corner of your game board. Next to this first tunnel, write "Start."

**2** For the "Finish," unbend three paper clips so you have three arches, then poke the ends into the game board in the bottom left-hand corner. Poke them all the way through the cardboard and bend the ends against the back of the cardboard so they stay secure. At the end of the row of arches write "Finish." Draw a curvy line that travels around your game board, beginning at "Start" and ending at "Finish." This will be the path of your maze.

**3** With your pen or pencil, poke four or five holes into your game board alongside the path you just drew, just a bit to one side or the other. Space them out all along the path. Wiggle your finger inside each hole to make them big enough to catch a marble temporarily, but not so big that the marble falls all the way in! These will be your "bottomless holes."

**4** Make one or two more cylinder tunnels and glue the ends together, then glue them onto different places along your path. Using several more paper clips, build a few more arches along your path. It doesn't matter where the tunnels and arches are placed—you can make your maze as easy or as difficult as you want.

**5** Spread two or three small spots of glue off to the sides of your path, and place a little cotton on top of these spots. These will be your "sandpits," and they must be avoided at all costs!

## HOW TO PLAY

Now you're ready to play! The edges of the shoe box top will keep your marble on the board. Each arch and tunnel are worth two points, and the sandpits and bottomless holes are minus two points. Place a marble at "Start" and tilt the game board back and forth, trying to stay on the path while scoring points and avoiding the sandpits. When you reach "Finish," add up all your points. The player with the most points wins!

19

# KOOKY-GORIES

Godzilla, Frankenstein, the Creature from the Black Lagoon, Dr. Jekyll. What other monsters can you think of? See how many nutty things you can name in this silly category game!

## WHAT YOU'LL NEED

• two or more players

## HOW TO PLAY

**1** One person chooses a category, such as "Cartoon Characters" or "Famous Monsters." Going clockwise, each player takes a turn naming an item in the category, like "Bugs Bunny," "Donald Duck," "Tweetie Bird," and so on. If you can't think of one in 10 seconds, you're out!

**2** Listen carefully and remember what the other players say because if you repeat an item, you're out. The last player in gets to name the category for the next game!

**3** When you're ready for an extra challenge, try naming the items in a category from A to Z. For instance, if the category is "Animals," begin with "alligator," then "bear," "cat," "donkey," and so on. You must go in alphabetical order, and you can't skip any letters! Here are some more category ideas to get you started: archvillains, superheroes, famous real animals, dolls, countries that begin with the letter "S," types of desserts, and breakfast cereals.

# IN THE NEWS!

And you thought the news was strange enough already! Just wait until you hear the wacky news stories you and your friends will come up with when you play *this* game!

## WHAT YOU'LL NEED

• two or more players    • old newspaper    • pen or pencil

## HOW TO PLAY

**1** Choose an article out of the newspaper. It could be anything— a front-page story, a sports report, a movie review, or even a letter from "Dear Abby."

**2** Read through the story and cross out two or three words per sentence. Make sure you choose a mix of nouns, verbs, and adjectives. (Nouns are people, places, or things; verbs are action words; and adjectives are words that describe nouns.)

**3** Then ask the other players for new words to replace the crossed-out ones. Nouns replace nouns, names replace names, verbs replace verbs, and so on. Be creative! The crazier the words, the better!

**4** Write the replacement words directly above the crossed-out words.

**5** When all the old words have been replaced, read the story, using the new words. See what kind of nutty story you have now! For example, if the players replace the word "president" with "bumble bee," "visited" with "arm-wrestled," and "Smith" with "Frosty the Snowman" in one sentence, you might end up with, "Today the bumble bee flew to Borneo and arm-wrestled with Prime Minister Frosty the Snowman." It may not be news anymore, but it's just as outrageous and a lot more fun!

# POSTCARD PASSION

Take a few minutes to tell your friends and family back home how much you miss them with your personalized postcards!

## WHAT YOU'LL NEED

- large piece of poster board
- ruler (optional)
- scissors
- colorful markers
- several postcard stamps
- pen
- camera (optional)
- glue (optional)

**Never use scissors in a moving vehicle, especially a car, bus, or train. Cut out what you need before you leave.**

## BEFORE YOU LEAVE

Cut the poster board into several rectangles 4¼ by 6 inches. These will be your postcards.

## HOW TO PLAY

**1** On your trip, look for memorable places or landmarks that you can draw. When you see something worth remembering, draw a picture of it.

**2** Then, at your next destination, write a note, pop a stamp on it, address it, and send it to a buddy. It's that easy!

**3** If you can, take photos of the places you visit. Then when you stay over somewhere, take the film to an hour-developing shop. Once you get your photos back, glue them to the fronts of the postcards. Don't forget to add a personal note!

# 18 MOBILE PHONE

Who needs an expensive portable phone when you can play this great "telephone" game—and all you need are your buddies and some good gossip!

## WHAT YOU'LL NEED

• four or more players     • pen or pencil     • paper

## HOW TO PLAY

**1** To start, one player writes a story that is three to six sentences long. The story must include one person, one place, and one thing that he or she has seen on the trip. Outside of that, the story can be about anything! The player must keep this story a secret!

**2** The first player then leans over to the next player and whispers the story into his or her ear. You're only allowed to whisper the story *one* time, so whisper clearly and slowly!

**3** The next player then whispers the story to the next player, and so on until the last player has heard it. Then the last player says the story out loud. Compare it to the story that was written down, and you'll all be surprised at how much it has changed! (Now you know how rumors start at school!)

# PUZZLE CARDS

Here's a cool card game that's as much fun to make as it is to play. Create your own deck of cards with pictures from old magazines and see which player can find the pieces and put together the most puzzles!

## WHAT YOU'LL NEED

- two to four players
- old magazines
- 16 pieces of cardboard or other heavy paper, 8½ by 11 inches each
- scissors
- glue

> Never use scissors in a moving vehicle, especially a car, bus, or train. Cut out what you need before you leave.

## BEFORE YOU LEAVE

**1** Go through some old magazines, choosing pictures that fill a full page. You need at least 15 or 16 full-page pictures, so if you have four players, each should find four pictures; if you have three players, each should find five; and if you have only two players, each will need to find eight!

**2** Carefully cut or tear the pictures out of the magazines and glue them onto the pieces of cardboard or heavy paper.

**3** Cut each picture into four equal pieces. You should end up with 60 or 64 cards.

## HOW TO PLAY

**1** Choose one player to be the dealer. The dealer collects all the cards and shuffles them. Each player is dealt seven cards, and should go through his or her cards and group together any cards that are parts of the same picture.

**2** The dealer then puts the remaining cards facedown, and turns over the top card and places it next to the deck.

**3** Going in a circle, each player chooses to take either the faceup card or a new one from the deck. Then that player discards one card from his or her hand onto the faceup pile.

**4** Around and around it goes. Anytime players complete a puzzle by collecting all four of the cards from one picture, they place those cards in a separate pile and draw four new cards from the facedown deck.

**5** When all the cards are gone from the facedown deck, reshuffle all the cards from the faceup pile (except the top one), place them facedown, and keep playing. Here's how to determine a winner:

(two players): the first player to make five complete puzzles
(three players): the first player to make four complete puzzles
(four players): the first player to make three complete puzzles

Now play again! Or, think of another game to play with your new deck of cards!

# 20 LEAVE 'EM LAUGHING

Who can keep the straightest face? Find out in this sidesplitting game where the object is to make the other players laugh without cracking up yourself! Good luck, and may the biggest clown win!

## WHAT YOU'LL NEED

• two or more players
• paper
• pencil

## HOW TO PLAY

**1** The first player gets 30 seconds to do the silliest thing he or she can think of to try to make the others laugh: sing the alphabet in a crazy way, yodel nursery rhymes, or make goofy faces. Players get one point for each player they make laugh, and lose one for each time they laugh at themselves or someone else.

**2** Appoint one person to keep track of the score on a piece of paper. The scorekeeper can play the game, too. When it's his or her turn to make others laugh, someone else can keep score that round.

**3** Each player takes a turn to try to get everyone else to crack a giggle. The first person to reach 10 points wins!

## ONE STEP FURTHER

This is also a great game to play throughout the day. Before you leave, everyone in the car agrees that at any moment one of the players might spring a surprise-attack crazy act on the others. Each person can keep track of his or her points.

# THE ROADSIDE SCRAMBLER

Did you ever stop to think about how many different words you can make from the letters "vacation"? "Can," "tin," "not"—how about "action"? Now the race is on to see how many words you can make from the cities, streets, and signs you see along the way!

## WHAT YOU'LL NEED

- two or more players
- paper
- pen or pencil
- timer or watch with second hand

## HOW TO PLAY

**1** Pick someone to be the caller. (The caller can also play the game.) The caller calls out the first two words from the first sign he or she sees.

**2** The players write these two words down, and the race is on. Use the letters in the words to form as many new words as you can. For example, if the first sign the caller sees reads, "Loveland, Colorado: Next Exit," the caller announces "Loveland, Colorado." The players write down "Loveland, Colorado," and try to form smaller, new words, such as "road," "cove," "cave," "doodle," and others. Each letter in each word equals one point.

**3** After two minutes, the caller calls time. Everyone now adds up his or her points. The player with the most points wins!

# CARTOON FLIP BOOK

Here's how to create your own cartoon characters having their own zany adventures. Who knows—maybe *your* cartoon character will have its own Saturday morning TV show one day.

## WHAT YOU'LL NEED

• pens or pencils      • old, thick paperback book that your parents don't want (no library or school books!) or a pad of Post-It™ notes

## HOW TO PLAY

**1** Think of a really silly character and a series of actions he or she (or it!) can do. Keep it simple at first—you may even want to do this activity using only stick figures.

**2** In the bottom right corner of the first page of the paperback or the first Post-It™ note, draw the first scene of your character doing something silly, like slipping on a banana peel, doing a handstand on the stairs, skateboarding wildly, or chasing a cow around a tree.

**3** On each of the following right-hand pages, draw the same picture—almost! Each time you draw it, change it just a little bit, adding a little movement. For example, if your monkey man is slipping on a banana peel, on the next page you may have his hat start to fall off. On each page, the hat should get closer and closer to the ground. Keep adding to your "cartoon" until all the pages are filled or your character's action is complete. The blank pages in the book or notepad can be filled up later with additional cartoons.

**4** Now you're ready for the show. Flip through your "cartoon" quickly, trying not to skip pages as you go. Watch your character run, jump, or fly through the air!

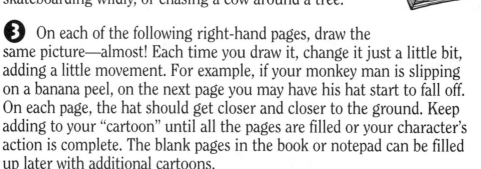

## ONE STEP FURTHER

Once you've completed one cartoon, do it again, using the *top* corner of the pages. And then, turn the book over and draw on the other sides of the pages.

# 23 EVERYBODY'S GOT A STORY

This never-ending story will provide never-ending fun for a long trip.

## WHAT YOU'LL NEED

- two or more players
- blank tape
- tape recorder with batteries
- stop watch or watch

## HOW TO PLAY

**1** One player begins the story with a single line, such as: "Once upon a time, there lived a lonely bubble gum collector." Each player then takes a turn adding one line to the story. There's just one catch—each player has to start his or her first line with the last word from the line before! So a story might go like this:

Player #1: "Once upon a time, there lived a lonely bubble gum collector…"
Player #2: "Collector Curt he was called, and he loved gum, especially peanut…"
Player #3: "Peanut butter gum and bananas were Curt's favorite breakfast…"

**2** Once everyone has had a turn, go back to the first player. Go around the group for a designated amount of time. (Usually three to five minutes works well.)

**3** Be sure to try tape recording your story—you'll get a laugh every time you hear it!

 # SENSATIONALLY SILLY STORIES

Test your creative writing skills by making up crazy stories with words you tear out of a magazine. See what kinds of tall tales you and your friends or siblings can come up with—but no fair trading words.

## WHAT YOU'LL NEED

- some old magazines
- glue stick
- large sheets of paper (one per player)

## HOW TO PLAY

**1** Carefully tear out 50 words from a magazine and lay them out on a sheet of paper. Find at least one word beginning with each letter of the alphabet.

**2** Arrange the words to make a short story. You don't have to use all of the words. Then, once you've laid the words out in the order you want, glue them down to the sheet of paper. This way, a nasty bump in the road won't send your story flying!

**3** Read your stories out loud to each other. The most clever one wins (all participants can vote to decide the winner).

## ONE STEP FURTHER

Try this game with teams—one team tears out 50 words for the other team and vice versa. Who can write the best (or most ridiculous) story? Have a parent judge. Tiebreakers can be decided based on which team was able to incorporate the most words into the story.

# WORD RACERS!

Can you find the hidden words? Do you think you could hide words so that no one else can find them? Here's your chance to find out in this do-it-yourself puzzle. You determine how hard it will be to solve!

## WHAT YOU'LL NEED

- two or more players
- scratch paper
- pen or pencil
- 8½-by-11-inch graph paper or 8½-by-11-inch plain paper and ruler (one per player)

## HOW TO PLAY

**1** Each player decides on his or her own secret subject, then chooses 10 words that are based on that subject (such as 10 kinds of animals, 10 flavors of ice cream, and 10 places to visit). Write them down on scratch paper, and don't show anyone!

**2** If you have graph paper, skip to the next step; otherwise, draw a big square on your sheet of 8½-by-11-inch plain paper. Then draw 12 lines going up and down and 12 lines going across, with about ½-inch space between each line. Make the lines as straight as you can, using a ruler if you have one. Now you have 121 boxes.

**3** Write each of your 10 words in connecting boxes (one letter in each box). Your words can go upward, downward, backward, forward, or even diagonally! Around all your words, write extra random letters so your original words are lost in a word puzzle. Then circle one of your hidden words as a hint about your subject.

**4** All the players trade puzzles, and the race is on! The first one to find all the hidden words and guess the subject wins.

# 26 SON OF HANGMAN

Here's a new twist on an old favorite!

## WHAT YOU'LL NEED

• two or more players    • paper    • pen or pencil

## HOW TO PLAY

**1** One player thinks of a phrase, famous saying, well-known name, or the title of a book or movie. On a piece of paper, the player then draws the same number of lines as there are letters in the phrase, just like Hangman or the TV show "Wheel of Fortune." Make sure to leave a space between each word. For example, if the phrase is "A fish out of water," the player would draw lines like this:

— — — — — — — — — — — — — — —

**2** Then, the player also thinks of a picture to draw that will give clues to the answer of the puzzle. The picture should have eight objects in it, and *no more than* eight. Using the phrase above, the player might decide to draw a picture of a dead-looking fish lying on a beach away from the water. The fish would be one object, the fish's eye another, the waves another, and so on.

**3** Now the game begins! The second player tries to solve the puzzle by guessing letters one at a time that are in the phrase. If the second player guesses correctly, the first player writes that letter in the correct place in the phrase. If the guess is incorrect, the first player draws one object of the picture. For example, let's say that after 10 turns, the second player has guessed "A - E - I - O - U - T - C - B - W - J." That's seven correct letters and three incorrect letters. The game now looks like this:

A _ I _ _  O U T  O _  W A T E _

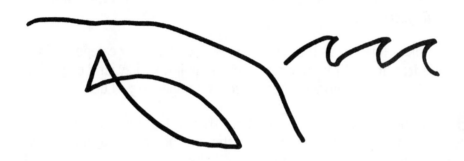

**4** The first player has drawn three objects of the picture, one for each miss. If the first player completes the picture before the second player guesses the phrase, the first player wins. But, if the second player guesses the phrase correctly first, he or she wins!

**5** Get it? Good! Then switch places so everyone gets a chance to guess and create a puzzle.

## 27 GET OFF MY BACK!

You'll have hours of back-to-back fun when you play this unique spelling and guessing game where you use each other's back as a blackboard. But beware: This game is not for the ticklish!

## WHAT YOU'LL NEED

• two players          • paper          • pen or pencil

## HOW TO PLAY

**1** Each player chooses a category, such as types of birds, words that start with "B," or parts of the body. Keep the category pretty simple, and *keep it to yourself!*

**2** Think of five things that would be included in your category. For types of birds, it might be sparrow, crow, blue jay, turkey, and eagle. You may want to write down your five objects on paper so you don't forget any!

**3** Once both players have figured out their categories and words, one player traces the first word, letter by letter, on the other player's back with his or her index finger. Pause a moment between each letter. You're only allowed to draw each letter in the word once, so go slowly and write big.

**4** Once the player has completed the word, the second player tries to figure it out, but keeps quiet about his or her guess (the second player can write it down if he or she wants to). The second player then turns around and writes a word from his or her chosen category on the back of the first player.

**5** Continue playing until both players have written all the words in the category on the other's back.

**6** Whoever figures out the category first wins. If neither player can figure out the category, or if both players figure it out at the same time, it's a tie, so play again. (In fact, even if it's not a tie, why not play again?)

# THE NAME GAME

Here's a terrific name game in which you have to pay close attention to all of the questions and all of the answers. Put all the clues together and see if you can guess who your mystery person is!

## WHAT YOU'LL NEED

• two or more players        • a pen or pencil        • 3-by-5-inch index cards

## HOW TO PLAY

**1** Each player writes down five famous names, each one on a separate index card. Famous names work the best, but they don't have to be real—try characters from cartoons or books.

**2** Everyone draws one name from the person on his or her left, but *without looking* at it!

**3** The players then hold the name they chose up to their foreheads so all the other players can see the name they picked.

**4** Going around in a circle, each player takes a turn asking one question about the name he or she selected. Only yes or no questions are allowed. Examples: "Is the person a man?" "Is the person make-believe?" "Does this person wear a cape?"

**5** Keep asking questions that are more and more exact to narrow down your person's identity. When you think you've got the answer, announce your identity. But be careful—two wrong guesses and you're out!

**6** The first player to guess correctly wins. Keep playing until all the names are used up. Then write some more and start again!

# FIVE IN A LINE

Are you bored with tic-tac-toe? This game is much more challenging, and you can play it with up to four (or even more!) players.

## WHAT YOU'LL NEED

- two or more players
- pen or pencil

- 8½-by-11-inch graph paper or 8½-by-11-inch plain paper and ruler

## HOW TO PLAY

**1** First, you need to draw your game board. On a piece of paper, draw a large box. Inside the box, use a ruler to draw lines running vertically and horizontally, each line about ½ inch from the other. You'll end up with a game board made up of a box with a few hundred squares. If you have graph paper, you can use the squares already printed.

**2** The object of the game is to be the first player to get "five in a line." It's played a little like tic-tac-toe, but it's on a much bigger board and you need to get *five* in a row—up and down, across, or diagonally. Also, you can play with more than two players.

**3** The rules are simple, but the strategy is complicated, so stay alert! After you decide who goes first, players take turns writing the first letter of their first name in any square, one square per turn, trying to be the first to get five initials in a row. If two of the players have the same initial, one of the players should use the first and second letters of his or her first name. Be sure to watch what the other players are doing, because you may have to play defense and block their rows.

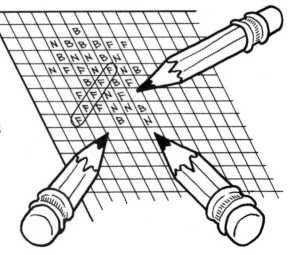

**4** Play until one of the players gets "five in a line," or until all the squares are filled. Then draw up another game board and play again!

# FACE RACE

Find out who the best artist is in this hilarious portrait game! Whether or not your pictures even look human, it's lots of fun.

## WHAT YOU'LL NEED

- two or more players
- pen or pencil
- paper
- hard surface
- colored pencils or pens (optional)

## HOW TO PLAY

**1** Each player has four minutes to draw a person that the other players know. It can be a famous person, such as a past president or a movie star, a cartoon or other fictional character, or someone in your town, such as a teacher or minister.

**2** Be as detailed as possible. For example, if the person you are drawing has a distinguishing feature, such as a wart, a pointy beard, or a baseball cap that's seemingly attached to his or her head, be sure to add that to the picture. It'll make it easier for the other players to guess, and everyone will think you're a great artist!

**3** Take turns guessing who the other players drew. Whoever identifies the most people in the pictures wins. And when you're done, give the pictures to the people you've drawn!

# BATLESS BASEBALL

Calling all baseball fans! Here's how to play a few games without a bat, ball, glove, or field! All you need are a pair of dice—and your imagination!

## WHAT YOU'LL NEED

- pair of dice
- pen or pencil
- a little baseball knowledge
- paper

## HOW TO PLAY

**1** First of all, draw up a score box like this:

| NAME | INNINGS | | | | | | | | |
|------|---|---|---|---|---|---|---|---|---|
| | 1 | 2 | 3 | 4 | 5 | 6 | 7 | 8 | 9 |
| MIKE | | | | | | | | | |
| TIM | | | | | | | | | |

**2** Play by yourself or with another player. If you're the only player, you roll for both teams. If there are two of you, roll to decide which one is the visiting team. The lowest roll is the visiting team and bats first. Write your team names in the space in the score box. Use your own names or make them up!

**3** Whoever is at bat has control of the dice. The number on the dice determines what the batter does at bat. Follow the key below:

2 = home run        6 = fly OUT to center    10 = fly OUT to right
3 = single          7 = single               11 = double
4 = walk            8 = strike OUT           12 = triple
5 = ground OUT to third   9 = ground OUT to second

**4** To start the game, the player at bat rolls the dice. The player keeps rolling the dice until his or her team gets three outs. Then he or she enters the score in the inning box, and the next player "goes to bat."

**5** Make sure to keep careful track of the runners on base and the runs scored by calling out the status of the game after each dice roll. For example, if you rolled a 7, 8, 3, and 10, you would say, "Runners on first and second, no runs, two outs." You can also write down each play to help keep track. One important rule to remember: no base stealing allowed!

**6** Play nine innings, and see who wins! If the game is tied, go into extra innings. Batter up!

# THE STORY OF YOUR LIFE

If you've ever thought about writing your life's story, here's how you can write the craziest autobiography of all time!

## WHAT YOU'LL NEED

- scissors
- pen or pencil
- several sheets of paper
- flat, hard surface

---

**Never use scissors in a moving vehicle, especially a car, bus, or train. Cut out what you need before you leave.**

---

## BEFORE YOU LEAVE

Cut up several long strips of paper, at least 30 to 40 strips. The strips should be at least an inch wide and long enough to write a whole sentence. Store these in your travel supply box until your trip.

## HOW TO PLAY

**1** Take your strips of paper and pen and start writing the story of your life. Use a strip of paper for each new sentence. Include where you were born, important and funny things that have happened to you, information about your family, and anything else that's meaningful to you.

**2** Now here's the twist. Once you are finished with your life story, throw all the sentences into a hat or your travel supply box. Mix them up, and pick out one line at a time. Place them down on a flat surface in the order you picked them out.

**3** Grab an audience and read your story. Be sure to read it in the order you picked the sentences. You can bet it's going to be goofy! You might even be born after you started school!

## ONE STEP FURTHER

Try this game with any story or fairy tale you can think of, and see what crazy tales you will create!

# MUTANT PAPER DOLL PUPPETS

Would your ears look better if they were attached to your elbows? How about a foot coming out of your forehead? Here's your chance to redesign the human body—make it as silly or as sensible as you want!

## WHAT YOU'LL NEED

- lightweight cardboard (such as old telephone book covers)
- a magazine or two
- scissors
- glue
- tape
- popsicle sticks or pencils
- lap desk (optional)

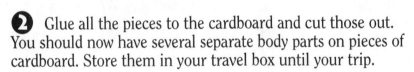

**Never use scissors in a moving vehicle, especially a car, bus, or train. Cut out what you need before you leave.**

## BEFORE YOU LEAVE

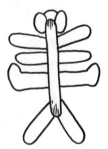

**1** Cut out pages from magazines that have pictures of people or parts of the body. Choose faces, arms, legs, feet, and so on, in all different sizes. Cut out the individual body parts.

**2** Glue all the pieces to the cardboard and cut those out. You should now have several separate body parts on pieces of cardboard. Store them in your travel box until your trip.

## HOW TO PLAY

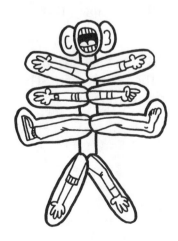

**1** On your lap or lap desk, arrange selected cut-out body parts any wacky way you want. Give your creature eight arms, toes instead of fingers—anything goes!

**2** Tape or glue the body parts together on a popsicle stick or pencil, as shown. Make a whole army of mutants!

**3** Finally, put on goofy mutant alien plays for each other!

# TRAVEL PASSWORD

This fun word game is sure to increase your vocabulary as you and a teammate compete for the grand password prize.

## WHAT YOU'LL NEED

- four or more players
- 3-by-5-inch index cards
- hat
- pen or pencil
- sheet of paper

## HOW TO PLAY

**1** Divide into two teams, Team A and Team B. Each team then writes down on an index card what it wants if it wins the game. (The teams should keep their prize cards a secret.) A prize might be "Get a foot massage from the losers," "Watch the losers feed each other ice cream while blindfolded," or anything else you can think of. But be careful—these "password prizes" are put in a hat and mixed up, so if you lose, you may end up having to act out your own "prize"!

**2** Now Team A and Team B each write down five words—two nouns, two verbs, and one adjective—on separate index cards. Then Team A players put their cards facedown in front of Team B, and vice versa.

**3** To begin the game, one player on Team A takes a card from the deck in front of his or her team. This player gives one-word hints to his or her team partners, trying to get them to guess the word written on the card. Here's the catch: Only noun hints may be given for nouns, verb hints for verbs, and adjective hints for adjectives. And you can't use any form of the word in your hint! For example, let's say the word on the card is "run," a verb. The verb hints might be "sprint," "dash," "jog," "race," and "hustle."

**4** For every hint a player gives, the teammates have to take one guess at the answer. Each wrong guess adds one point to the team's score. The maximum number of clues that can be received on a word is five.

**5** After a correct guess or five clues, write down the points.
Here's how to determine the score:

> If the word is guessed after the first clue, you receive no points.
> If the word is guessed after the second clue, you receive one point.
> If the word is guessed after the third clue, you receive two points.
> If the word is guessed after the fourth clue, you receive three points.
> If the word is guessed after the fifth clue, you receive four points.

**6** Now a member from Team B takes a card and tries to get the Team B players to guess the word. After each team goes through five words, add up the score. In this game, the team with the *least* number of points wins! Don't forget to let the winning team pick the password prize from the hat.

# ON-THE-SPOT DOT-TO-DOT

You don't need to be an incredible artist to create great works of dot-to-dot art! Make your own dot-to-dot puzzles, then give it to a younger brother or sister who just can't seem to sit still. (Your parents will be forever in your debt!)

## WHAT YOU'LL NEED

- favorite magazine with pictures
- pen or pencil
- tracing paper

## HOW TO PLAY

**1** Find a picture in your magazine that you want to use for your dot-to-dot puzzle. Try using a picture of a famous person or building.

**2** Put the paper on top of the picture and trace over it. Don't use straight or crooked lines, just dots. Be careful not to make the dots too close together; otherwise, your sibling will guess the picture before he or she even does the activity. Leave about ½ inch to 1 inch between each dot.

**3** Once you have finished outlining the picture with dots, number the dots, starting with 1 and continuing on, assigning each dot a consecutive number.

**4** Now give it to a younger brother or sister to connect the dots. Can he or she guess the picture you traced? Who cares? It's great fun—and it keeps him or her out of your hair!

# 36 NAMES-OF-FAME CHAIN

Here's a game that will test your knowledge of famous people, whether they're real or make-believe! The biggest name-dropper wins!

## WHAT YOU'LL NEED

• two or more players

## HOW TO PLAY

**1** One player starts by naming a famous person in history, the movies, rap music, books, or anything else you can think of.

**2** The next player must name another famous person whose first name starts with the first letter of the last name of the previous famous person. Confused? Don't be—it's easy! If the first person says "George Washington," the next person has to say "William Shakespeare" or another name starting with "W."

**3** Then the following person has to say "Sylvester Stallone" or another "S" name. Remember, they don't have to be real people, just famous names! Even "Roger Rabbit" will do! See how many names you can connect together, but if you can't think of one, you're out!

WAYNE GRETZKY.

..."G"... THAT'S EASY... UM... UHH... WELL...

# WHAT'S THE WORD?

Here's another word game that will have you under its "spell." Can you fill in the missing letters and guess the word before the other players do?

## WHAT YOU'LL NEED

- two or more players
- dictionary
- paper
- pen or pencil

## HOW TO PLAY

**1** Choose one player to be the "Word Master." That player looks up a word and its definition in the dictionary. Long, uncommon words are best, but make sure the word is not *too* impossible!

**2** The Word Master writes the word on a piece of paper, leaving out the first letter and every other letter after that. He or she also underlines the spaces where the missing letters belong.

**3** Next, the Word Master writes a one- or two-word definition below the word. For example, if the player chooses the word "cantankerous," he or she would write "_ A _ T _ N _ E _ O _ S" and underneath it would write "bad-tempered."

**4** With more than two players, the players take turns guessing letters to fill in the missing spaces. One correct letter guess fills in only one space, so you can guess the same letter more than once.

**5** Each correct guess is worth one point and another turn. After a wrong guess, it's the next player's turn.

**6** Continue taking turns guessing letters. The player who figures out the word first and correctly guesses it receives five points. Any player who guesses at the word and gets it wrong loses two points and his or her turn.

**7** After five rounds with five different words, add up the scores. The one with the most points wins and becomes the next Word Master. Now play again!

## ONE STEP FURTHER

Once everyone becomes a Word Master extraordinaire, try the game with whole phrases instead of words. Like this: " _ N / _ P _ L _ / A / _ A _ / K _ E _ S / _ H _ / D _ C _ O _ / A _ A _." The hint: "medical advice." Can you guess what it is?

47

# 38 DO YOU REMEMBER?

- - - - - - - - - - - - - - - - - - - - -

Do you have a photographic memory? Find out with this game that gives your travel-weary brain cells a real workout!

## WHAT YOU'LL NEED

- two or more players
- shoe box or paper bag
- several sheets of paper
- 15 small items per player
- pens or pencils (one per player)
- watch or clock with a second hand
- travel supply box

## HOW TO PLAY

**1** First, everyone collects 15 different small items and stores them in a shoe box or paper bag. You can do this either before you leave or on the road. Make sure to keep your items secret from everyone else! Some possible items: small shiny rocks, coins, leaves, spools of thread, flowers, napkins, and erasers. (Unusual items are especially good to collect, but please, no bugs!)

**2** Hand out paper and pencils or pens to everyone. Pick one player to spread all of his or her items on the lid of the travel supply box so that everyone can see them. After 30 seconds, the player then puts the items back into the bag or box.

**3** Now each player has two minutes to write down as many of the items as he or she can remember. No fair peeking at anyone else's list!

**4** After the time is up, the person with the objects takes the items out of the bag or box one at a time. The players should give themselves a point for each correct object that is written down. The player with the most correctly listed items wins!

**5** Now let the next player put his or her items in the lid, and start the game again!

# AUTO-BIOGRAPHY

Use long hours spent traveling in a car to create a story that you not only write, but illustrate, too!

## WHAT YOU'LL NEED

- several sheets of paper
- old magazine
- pen or pencil
- glue
- stapler or tape
- photo of yourself (optional)

## HOW TO PLAY

**1** Go through an old magazine, looking for pictures to illustrate the things that have happened in your life. Choose pictures of babies, houses, schools, and so on.

**2** Tear out each picture carefully, and use them in place of words you would write. You can write a few words, then paste in a picture. For instance, the first line of your story may be, "When I was a little girl, I couldn't even tie my own shoes." Then, you'd find a picture of a girl and some shoes and *replace* the pictures with the words.

**3** Keep on writing and finding pictures, tearing them out, and pasting them on consecutive pieces of paper, until you've finished your story. Soon you will have a fully illustrated story about you!

**4** Finally, make your story into a real book by binding the left side of the pages with staples or tape (make sure your pages are in the correct order). Name your story and illustrate a cover. Don't forget to paste in a photo of yourself!

# MYSTERY MESSAGES

Have you ever wanted to get a message to your brothers, sisters, or friends that only they could read? Here's a way! Only someone with the code breaker (that you create!) will be able to figure out your "top secret information."

## WHAT YOU'LL NEED

- two or more players
- old magazines
- sheet of paper
- pen or pencil
- glue or tape

## HOW TO PLAY

**1** Think of a message to send, such as: "Meet me at the motel pool at 5 P.M.," "Let's ditch Michelle at the truck stop," or "Brian has termites."

**2** Find the words you need in a magazine and carefully tear them out.

**3** Scramble the words and arrange them on a piece of paper. Now, your message might read something like this: "motel P.M. at meet pool me the 5 at."

**4** Glue or tape the words on the paper and write a number to the right of each word. For example, the message would now read: "motel (1) P.M. (2) at (3) meet (4) pool (5) me (6) the (7) 5 (8) at (9)". Feel safe passing the message around, because no one will know what it means—yet!

**5** Next, write the code breaker that only you and your chosen pal will have access to. To do this, write down the numbers that are next to the words in the order that the words *should* read. For example, the code breaker for the message illustrated here would read: "4 6 3 7 1 5 9 8 2."

**6** Then, give the code breaker to your co-conspirator. Once he or she has both the coded message and the code breaker, your co-conspirator can put the two together to figure out the message.

# BRAT CAGE

When, after hours on the road, your bratty little brother and sister are driving you crazy, use this "cage" to tame their pesky personalities!

## WHAT YOU'LL NEED

• photo of your brother or sister (or any other brat!)
• scissors
• cardboard

• yarn, about 4 feet
• glue
• pencil or markers

> **Never use scissors in a moving vehicle, especially a car, bus, or train. Cut out what you need before you leave.**

## BEFORE YOU LEAVE

Cut the cardboard into a circle big enough to fit the photo on. Poke two holes, one on each end of the cardboard. Cut the yarn into two pieces, each about 2 feet long.

## HOW TO PLAY

**1** On one side of the cardboard, draw a box and five thick black lines going across from top to bottom. These are the "bars" to the prison.

**2** Glue the photo to the other side of the cardboard.

**3** Thread one piece of yarn into one of the holes on the cardboard, then tie the yarn in a loop. Do the same with the other side. This should give you a loop of yarn on both ends of the circle.

**4** Next, hold the ends of the yarn in your hands. Twirl the cardboard circle around and around to wind it up, then pull the two pieces of yarn outward so the cardboard circle spins around. As the circle flips around, the alternating photo and "bars" will make it look as if you have the pesky person locked up in a cage!

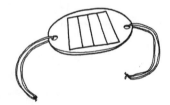

# 42  PUT YOUR TRIP ON THE MAP QUIZ

Here's a terrific way to draw cool maps, play a game, and remember your journey—all at the same time.

## WHAT YOU'LL NEED

• two players          • paper          • pen or pencil

## HOW TO PLAY

**1** To start, both players need a piece of paper and a pen or pencil. You draw the map first and the other player is the quiz contestant.

**2** Begin by drawing a map of what you see as you travel. Don't leave out anything—big cross streets, highways, bridges, rivers, lakes, mountains, and buildings. Draw quickly, but accurately. Make any notes you think might be important, such as city names, landmarks, or even interesting scenery you pass.

**3** At the same time, the other player takes notes on what he or she sees along the way, concentrating on as many landmarks and as much scenery as possible.

**4** After approximately 20 minutes, or after drawing 30 to 40 sites, stop drawing. Then make a neat copy of the map you've just drawn. Only this time, write in the names of only half the landmarks and other map entries, and draw in blank lines next to other half (at least 20) of the sites. These blanks will be filled in by the quiz taker.

**5** Now hand the map with the blanks to the other player. Using only his or her notes, the quiz taker must fill in the names of the landmarks in the blanks. Here's how to score your quiz:

> 16 to 20 correct: Excellent! Consider a career in navigation!
> 11 to 15 correct: Very good! You could lead the expedition.
> 6 to 10 correct: Not so hot. Back to map school!
> 0 to 5 correct: Watch out—you might get lost in your own backyard!

**6** Now switch positions and play again!

# 43 WHAT AN ANIMAL!

Have your parents or teachers ever told you to "stop acting like an animal?" It's usually a good idea, *except* when you're playing this game!

## WHAT YOU'LL NEED

- four or more players
- scratch paper
- pen or pencil
- 2 hats or small boxes

## HOW TO PLAY

**1** Divide into two teams. Each team writes down the names of 10 animals on 10 small scraps of paper. Pick animals that are a little out of the ordinary, such as an orangutan or a crocodile.

**2** When the teams are finished, each should place the scraps of paper into two different hats or boxes. It is important to keep the teams' animals separate from each other.

**3** To begin, one player from one team chooses a piece of paper from the other team's hat or box. Without saying anything, he or she must act like the animal written on the paper and try to get his or her teammates to guess that animal.

**4** If the teammates are having a difficult time figuring out the animal, the player can also make animal sounds. Each team receives three points for guessing the animal if no sounds are made, and one point if sounds are used. Whichever team earns the most points wins.

# LICENSE PLATE LOTTO

You may not win millions of dollars with this version of lotto, but you'll win your friends' admiration when you're the lotto champion!

## WHAT YOU'LL NEED

- three or more players
- pen or pencil
- ruler
- scratch paper
- several pieces of light-colored construction paper (at least one per player)

## PREPARING THE GAME BOARD

**1** First, you need to make a game board for each player. To make a board, take a sheet of construction paper. Use a ruler to draw six lines across and six lines vertical, with about an inch space between each line. This should give you 25 squares.

**2** Now each player fills in each box with a letter. Any letter of the alphabet can be used, but a letter can't be used more than twice on one board.

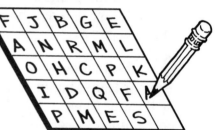

## HOW TO PLAY

**1** Choose one person to be the caller. Mix up all the game boards, and give one to each player except the caller. The players should also have a piece of scratch paper that they can tear into small pieces.

**2** When the caller sees a passing car, he or she will announce the first letter on the license plate. So, if the license plate reads "2XRT436," the letter called would be "X."

**3** Any player with that letter on his or her board, tears off a small piece of scratch paper and covers the spot. Only one letter can be covered per call, so if the letter called is "A" and you have two "A's" on your board, you can cover only one of them.

**4** The first player to cover all the letters and fill the game board wins! Be sure the winner shouts "LPL!" (License Plate Lotto).

**5** The winner now becomes the caller, and you can start the game all over again.

# LOONY TUNE-Y

While this game may not lead you into a career in music, it will definitely lead you to laughter!

## WHAT YOU'LL NEED

• two or more players     • pen or pencil     • paper

## HOW TO PLAY

**1** To start, all the players agree on a familiar tune, such as "Happy Birthday."

**2** Once that's decided, everyone writes down his or her own funny new words to the song. All the verses should be about family members, teachers, friends, or someone else that everybody in the group knows—even your dog!

**3** Go around in a circle and let each player take a turn singing his or her own unique version. Each player should sing only a verse or two so that the game moves along quickly.

**4** Want an example? Pretend the lyrics are about a friend named Joe, and the melody is from the song "Row, Row, Row Your Boat." The song could go something like this:

*Joe, Joe, Joe is twelve;*
*He thinks he's really cool;*
*Terribly, terribly, terribly, terribly;*
*He's rather quite a fool!*

Silly enough for you? Start singing!

# STUMP A STRANGER

**PARENTAL SUPERVISION REQUIRED**

Here are three wacky word gags! Have a contest with your brother or sister to see who can stump the most people.

## WHAT YOU'LL NEED

• two or more players          • paper          • pen

## HOW TO PLAY

**1** The gags listed below have been around a long time. You get five points for each gag you pull off successfully. If the person guesses the joke correctly, you receive one point for getting the person to play along. You must take turns with your opponents.

**2** The only rule in this game is that you can ask only one person one of the gags. Otherwise, that person is likely to catch on to the gags. You can ask a server at a restaurant, a gas station attendant, cousins you visit, anyone! *However, never approach a stranger by yourself.* A parent should be with you at all times.

**3** When you find someone to play the game with, always ask the person first if he or she has a minute for a good gag. If the person doesn't have time, don't bother him or her.

### GAG 1

You begin by saying "Say stop." The other person says "Stop." You say "Say go." The other person says "Go." Repeat this about five times or so, keeping a rapid pace. Then, when the other person expects you to say "Say stop," you say "What do you do at a green light?" Usually, the person will say "Stop" and you got 'em!

- - - - - - - - - - - - - - - - - - - - - - -

## GAG 2

You say "Say toast," and the person says "Toast." You say "Say most," and the person says "Most." Once again, you'll want to repeat these about five times or so at a quick pace. Then, instead of saying "Say toast" again, you say "What do you put in the toaster?" The person will probably say "Toast!" And you say "Nope, you put bread in a toaster!"

## GAG 3

You say "Say black." The person says "Black." You say "Say white." The person says "White." Repeat this a few times, and then say "What do cows drink?" You can bet the person will say, "Milk!" And you say "Nope, cows don't drink milk, they give it!"

## ONE STEP FURTHER

After you've done the gags listed for a while, make up some of your own!

# BOMBS AWAY

Destroy your enemy's buildings before your enemy destroys yours in this wild war game! You don't have to be a military genius to play, but victory will go to the player with the most accurate bombers.

## WHAT YOU'LL NEED

- two players
- pen or pencil

- 8½-by-11-inch graph paper or 8½-by-11-inch plain paper and ruler

## PREPARING FOR THE GAME

**1** Each player needs his or her own blueprint to "build" a city. If graph paper isn't available, draw 11 lines down and 11 lines across on your paper to make 100 squares. The lines should be about ½ inch apart.

**2** Number the columns of squares going down (1 through 10) and assign letters (A through J) to the rows going across. Write "Home Base" across the top of the paper.

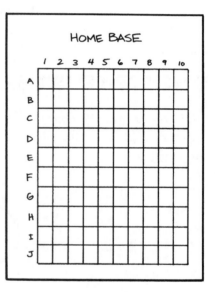

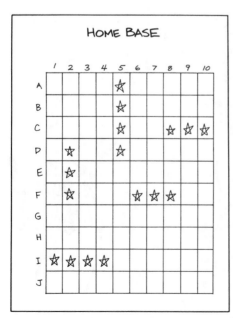

**3** Each player gets five buildings to draw in. Draw in three buildings that take up three squares each and two that use four squares each. Place them anywhere you like in your city. They can go up and down or sideways (not diagonally). Mark the placement of your buildings with stars, as the picture here shows. Important: Don't let your opponent see your map!

58

## HOW TO PLAY

**1** The object of the game is to bomb all of your opponent's buildings that are marked on his or her map. To begin, Player One calls out a letter/number combination, such as "4-A." If Player Two has a star drawn in that square, he says, "On target," and places an "X" in that square on his board. At the same time, Player One draws an "X" in that square on her board to represent a hit. But, if Player One calls out a letter/number combination, and none of Player Two's buildings are in that square, it's a miss, and Player Two says, "Off target." Player Two doesn't mark anything on his board, but Player One marks her miss with a big "O" on her board in the appropriate spot.

**2** Players continue taking turns, answering "On target" for a hit and "Off target" for a miss, and keeping track on the charts. If Player One wipes out all the sections in one of Player Two's buildings, Player Two says, "Out of action." (See the example in the illustration in row I, columns 1 through 4.)

**3** The player to wipe out all of his or her opponent's buildings first is the winner! Bombs away!

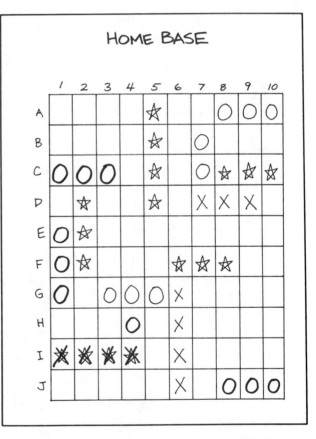

# THUMPER

Ready to make some noise as you sharpen your memory and your coordination? This game will have you clapping, singing, gesturing, and thumping until you find yourselves abandoned at a rest stop just outside Okoboji!

## WHAT YOU'LL NEED

• three or more players

## HOW TO PLAY

**1** Each player chooses a gesture that will be his or her gesture. For example, with three players:

#1 may choose grabbing his or her ears
#2 may choose clapping his or her hands
#3 may choose covering his or her eyes

**2** Then all players agree on one "transition" gesture, like holding their noses. Choose one player to be "It." This person will start the game.

**3** Now, everyone starts drumming on their thighs—THUMPING—and . . .

"It": "What's the name of the game?"
Other players: "THUMPER!"
"It": "How do you play it?"
Other players: "Thump it!"

**4** Then "It" does his or her gesture, followed by the "transition" gesture, followed by another player's gesture. The player whose gesture came last goes next, and on it goes. Here's an example:

"It" grabs his ears, then holds his nose, and finally, claps his hands. Clapping hands is #2's gesture, so #2 then claps her hands, holds her nose, then covers her eyes. Covering eyes is #3's gesture, so #3 covers his eyes, then holds his nose, and either grabs his ears or claps his hands.

All the while, the players keep thumping their thighs with their hands. Whoever misses a gesture, gets a gesture in the wrong order, or forgets one is out. You can go in any order, and you can even pick yourself! See how fast you can go, and have a THUMPING good time!

# ARMCHAIR FOOTBALL

If you like the fast action of football, you'll love this version of football played with dice! Go for the bomb, run back a kickoff, block a punt, and score, score, score! You can play by yourself or with another fan!

## WHAT YOU'LL NEED

- small piece of cardboard
- scissors
- paper
- pair of dice
- ruler
- pen or pencil
- a little football knowledge

**Never use scissors in a moving vehicle, especially a car, bus, or train. Cut out what you need before you leave.**

## BEFORE YOU LEAVE

Cut out a ball marker and a first-down marker from cardboard. The ball marker should be a triangle, and the first-down marker should be a rectangle exactly 1 inch wide.

## PREPARING FOR THE GAME

❶ First, you need to prepare your field. With a ruler, draw a large rectangle on a piece of paper and mark off the end zones and all the 10-yard lines. Each 10-yard line should be 1 inch apart.

G  10  20  30  40  50  40  30  20  10  G

ENDZONE · · · · · · · · · · ◁ BALL · · · · ENDZONE

1ST DOWN

Also draw in the "hash marks." Those are the short lines that mark every yard on the field.

❷ Now draw a scoreboard on a separate sheet of paper. It should look like this:

| TEAM | 1 | 2 | 3 | 4 | FINAL |
|------|---|---|---|---|-------|
|      |   |   |   |   |       |
|      |   |   |   |   |       |

# HOW TO PLAY

**1** Here are three rules to remember and to read at the start of the game: 1) If a play goes past the end zone (such as a 60-yard pass from the 20-yard line), it's a touchdown; 2) if a punt goes into the end zone, it's a touchback and comes out to the return team's 20-yard line; and 3) if a field goal is no good, the defensive team immediately receives the ball where it lays (this is called the line of scrimmage).

**2** Refer to the following charts for all the plays. The number on the left stands for the sum of the two dice rolled for each play. You may want to copy these charts onto separate pieces of paper for easy reference.

## RUN

2 = TOUCHDOWN!
3 = Big hole! 10-yard gain
4 = 3-yard loss
5 = 4-yard gain
6 = Big pile up! 2-yard gain
7 = 6-yard loss
8 = 5-yard gain
9 = Stopped cold! No gain
10 = Good move! 17-yard gain
11 = No blocking! 5-yard loss
12 = 25-yard gain

## PUNT

2-4 = 20 yards
5-6 = 60 yards
7-8 = 45 yards
9-12 = 30 yards

## FIELD GOAL

2-7 = Blocked! Other team gains control
8-12 = Good! (Player must be at least at his or her own 40-yard line to attempt a field goal)

## PASS

2 = Bomb! 60-yard gain
3 = Intercepted—it's the other team's ball at the 50
4 = On target! 15-yard gain
5 = Incomplete pass
6 = 10-yard gain
7 = Stopped cold! No gain
8 = Incomplete pass
9 = Sack! 8-yard loss
10 = Incomplete pass
11 = Post pattern! 20-yard gain
12 = Bomb! 40-yard gain

## KICKOFF RETURN

2 = Down the sideline! TOUCHDOWN
3-4 = Returned to return team's 40-yard line
5-9 = Returned to return team's 20-yard line
10-12 = Returned to return team's 30-yard line

**3** Now you're ready to play. Flip a coin to see who kicks off and who receives. Then each player takes one dice, and the game is on. If you're playing alone, you'll roll both dice (for the offense and defense). To kick off, both players roll their dice and use the "Kickoff Return" chart to see where to place the ball. Point the ball marker to the spot and place the edge of the first-down marker along the sideline, beginning at that spot as well. This will show the offensive team how far he or she needs to go to get a first down.

**4** Next, the offensive player announces if the next play is going to be a run or a pass. Both players roll their dice and check either the "Run" chart or the "Pass" chart. For instance, the offensive player calls a run and the roll of both dice equals a five. This gives the offensive team a four-yard gain, so the player should move the ball marker up four yards to mark the spot. Now it's second down and six yards to go for the first down. If the next play is a pass and the roll is a ten, the offense has an incomplete pass. Now it's third down, and there are still six yards to go for a first down.

**5** Each quarter lasts for 20 plays, so keep a count of the plays on the sheet of paper that has the scoreboard. Kickoffs and punts also count as plays. Drive up the field, punt, kick a field goal, or score a touchdown! At the end of each quarter, write in the score on your scoreboard. Play hard, play clean, and may the best team win!

# 50 BUSINESS CARD BONANZA!

You and your pals will mean business when it comes to seeing who can win this collector's game!

## WHAT YOU'LL NEED

• small box or paper sack

## HOW TO PLAY

**1** The object of this game is to see who can collect the most business cards and free memorabilia during your trip. Make sure that all participants understand the rules below, then start collecting!

**2** Every place you go, tuck a business card, restaurant napkin, or a hotel and entertainment brochure into your box or sack. Each of these items count as one point. You cannot count any item that you paid for, and you cannot take anything that is not supposed to be given away, such as ashtrays or hotel towels.

**3** As you collect the souvenirs, try to be secretive. If all the participants see what everyone else is taking, then everyone will end up with the same items. Keep all your items hidden away.

**4** Once you get home, or reach a certain destination in your journey, everyone should count up all the business cards, napkins, brochures, and other free memorabilia he or she has collected. Whoever has the most wins! (But in "Business Card Bonanza," everyone really wins, because everyone ends up with loads of free souvenirs from every place visited!)